ARCHITECTURE & DESIGN LIBRARY

ART DECO

ARCHITECTURE & DESIGN LIBRARY

ART DECO

Young Mi Kim

FRIEDMAN/FAIRFAX
PUBLISHERS

A FRIEDMAN/FAIRFAX BOOK

© 1997 by Michael Friedman Publishing Group, Inc.

Library of Congress Cataloging-in-Publication Data

Kim, Young Mi, date
    Art deco / Young Mi Kim.
       p.   cm. — (Architecture & design library ; 5)
    Includes index.
    ISBN 1-56799-431-8
    1. Art deco—United States. 2. Art, Modern—20th century—United
States.   I. Title. II. Series: Architecture and design library ;
5.
    N6512.5.A7K56 1997
    709'73'09041—dc20   96-34082

Editor: Francine Hornberger
Art Director: Kevin Ullrich
Photography Editors: Samantha Larrance and Deidra Gorgos
Layout: Joan Pecolick
Production Manager: Camille Lee

Color separations by Colourscan Overseas Co Pte Ltd.
Printed and bound in China

1 3 5 7 9 10 8 6 4 2

For bulk purchases and special sales, please contact:
Friedman/Fairfax Publishers
Attention: Sales Department
15 West 26th Street
New York, New York 10010
212/685-6610 FAX 212/685-1307

Visit our website:
http://www.metrobooks.com

To my family and closest friends,
for giving me inspiration and perspective.
To Scott,
for providing me with love, encouragement, and humor
—even in the face of tight deadlines.

━━━━━━

My sincerest thanks to the Art Deco Society of Boston,
as well as the various Art Deco Clubs around the world,
for their dedication to this important genre.

C o n t e n t s

INTRODUCTION

During the 1920s, Modernists—the community of designers, architects, and artists who promoted simplicity of form and lack of ostentation—dismissed a new style introduced to North America by way of France. This style, called Art Deco, followed, at least on its surface, all of the Modernists' rules governing exteriors and interiors—save for one. Alas, the Art Deco style was fun.

So exuberant was this new aesthetic that it became the style of choice for many public buildings and places, including movie theaters, train stations, restaurants, hotels, and ocean liners. Yet, even with its commercial popularity, Art Deco in its time was the style scholars and Modernists loved to hate.

Today, that derision has turned to enthusiasm, as dozens of Art Deco societies have sprung up all over the world, Art Deco buildings continue to be granted landmark status, and growing numbers of enthusiasts collect furnishings from the era. And, as the ultimate sign of acceptance and appreciation, Art Deco is being used outside of the commercial and public spaces that popularized it: now, people are decorating their homes in the Art Deco style.

Except for a revival in the 1960s, Art Deco has never been more popular in America than it is today, perhaps because it embodies much more than a style of decoration. Historians, who still hotly debate its period of origin and existence, generally regard Art Deco as a movement that started in the 1920s that not only touched North American art, culture, and design, but left an indelible mark. And although named after the Parisian decorative arts exposition of 1925—and drawn from widely disparate styles and cultures—Art Deco has become uniquely American.

Anyone who has seen the ornamental spire atop the Chrysler Building in New York, or watched the film *Broadway Melody* (1938), has appreciated American Art Deco in two of its most enduring forms: architecture and celluloid. Its influence also lives in the posters of some of our best graphic artists, the works of some our most prominent sculptors, and even in some of our simplest household objects.

Indeed, Art Deco's impressions are unmistakable: stream-lined, rakish forms, geometric shapes, zigzags, seductive curves, and smooth

OPPOSITE: *In New York, the Chrysler Building stands as a monument to the greatness of Art Deco. Its ornamental spires, shown here, recall tribal influences and modernity all at once. Ziggurats, zigzags, triangles, and chevrons were common motifs used by architects of the day, usually to accommodate strict building codes. The stepped-back structure of the spire allowed this skyscraper to be built to its maximum height.*

ABOVE: *Radio City Music Hall in New York City is one of the most famous commercial examples of Art Deco. Erected at the height of the Art Deco movement, it still maintains its original exterior as well as interior design.*

surfaces are a few telltale signs. These and other motifs and themes that make up the style we now call Art Deco speak of an era in North America that, even at its most turbulent and changing, was always looking to the future for its influence.

In fact, Art Deco's greatest attribute may be its staying power: although it is thought to have originated around 1909 (the year the Ballets Russes arrived in Paris, enchanting French designers with its opulent sets and costumes), Art Deco had its heyday in the 1920s and '30s in America, and continued to influence architecture, furniture and industrial design throughout the 1940s, 1950s, and 1960s. Today, Art Deco designs from all decades continue to be revived and revered by devotees of this aesthetic.

Historians agree that some of the greatest landmarks of the twentieth century were built during the Art Deco era. Many North American landmarks come immediately to mind: San Francisco's Golden Gate Bridge, the Southwest's Hoover Dam, and Rockefeller Center, the Chrysler Building, and the Empire State Building, all of which are in New York City. Of course, some of the country's most public places—bus and train terminals—are legendary Deco buildings. These include Union Passenger Terminal (Los Angeles), Union Station (Omaha), 30th Street Station (Philadelphia), Union Depot (Tulsa), and Cincinnati Union Terminal.

One of the most remarkable Art Deco buildings in New York is Radio City Music Hall, whose interiors received landmark status in 1978. As the first building to be completed in Rockefeller Center, it employed a number of notable Art Deco artisans in its construction. René Chambellan was the architectural sculptor for the hall and Donald Deskey was its interior designer. Because of its landmark status, all the public areas of the theater, including the carpets, drapes, wall coverings, and furnishings have been maintained in their original design, fabric, color, and style.

LEFT: *Miami Beach's Marlin hotel is one of the best examples of "Tropical Deco." Elements such as ledges that curl around the sides of the building, a geometric frieze along the flat roof, and a highly stylized sans-serif sign above the entrance all tell of an Art Deco influence. Of course, smooth contours and use of glass show the building's Modernist roots.*

RIGHT: *In England, Art Deco's influence is abundantly apparent in architecture. Here, a nautical scene enlivens the ceiling of the Midland Hotel in Morecambe, England, which was built in the 1930s. The sculpted relief, titled Triton, was created by artist Eric Gill. Using artistry on the ceiling—which draws the eye upward—was a particular bent of Art Deco architects, many of whom liked to call attention to detailing.*

Deskey, who designed most of the Hall's furniture himself, continued to produce pieces for use in both commercial and residential spaces. Most of the furniture in Radio City Music Hall is widely regarded as classic examples of Art Deco design. The Hall's interiors have for many years served as a template of sorts for homeowners interested in capturing a Deco spirit in the home, from the rich carpet designs to the fabric colorways used in upholstered seating.

One reason why so many people are drawn to Art Deco is because of its rich historical context. It combines elements of Cubism and the Industrial Age, of the Jazz Age and the Great Depression. It takes motifs from the cultures of Japan, Mesopotamia, Egypt, and sub-Saharan Africa, as well as from the Mayan and Aztec cultures. Most importantly, it shows an appreciation for the polished, dynamic forms of modern-day machines, such as aircraft. Often referred to as Jazz Modern, Style Moderne, or Streamline Modern, Art Deco is anything but pure. Yet, its checkered background is the reason why this style continues to fascinate us: in it we see bits of our past, our present, and, perhaps, our future.

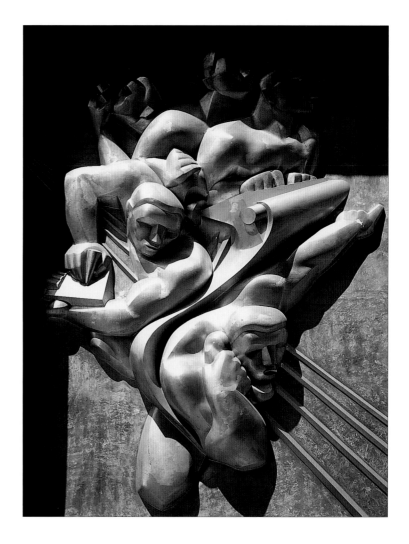

ABOVE: *At Rockefeller Center in New York City, this plaque, sculpted by Isamu Noguchi in 1939, is a fitting entrance to the Associated Press building. Its rounded, stylized figures and silvery appearance are testament to Art Deco's lasting impression on architecture and art in this city.*

A WORK IN PROGRESS

Although North American Art Deco household items are generally synonymous with mass production, the origins of Art Deco, ironically, lay in craft. During the early 1900s, French interior designers, furniture makers, and the big department stores were captivated with a highly ornamental furniture style that showcased expensive woods and exotic materials. Often, a small but wealthy clientele would commission a small series or a one-of-a-kind item.

North America got its first glimpse of this emerging style in 1926, when a massive exhibition of European decorative arts was presented by the Metropolitan Museum of Art. The show featured some of the best work displayed during the Parisian Exposition International des Arts Décoratifs et Industriels Modernes, which had taken place the prior year. The exhibition subsequently went to several major cities, gaining exposure and popularity along the way. In 1927, a commercial venture by the company that underwrote the exhibition—R.H. Macy—was wildly successful. In its "Moderne" boutique, Macy's exhibited and sold contemporary decorative arts to the public. Other large department stores promptly followed.

The style was quickly evolving. Eventually, it would combine many of the French motifs with the ideals of another school of thought emerging in Germany: Bauhaus. The philosophy of these Modernists, as they were called, impacted upon the creations of both French and American designers after 1925. Social forces were at work, too, in shaping the development of the style. It was a heady time, when North America struggled between two world wars and the Great Depression; when jazz came into popularity; and when Hollywood was at its most glamorous. Indeed, American Art Deco during its peak was truly a work in progress.

In the 1920s and '30s, Art Deco hit its peak. Made of modern and plentiful materials such as steel, and lacking the ornamentation of traditionally hand-carved or wrought pieces, many Art Deco household items were designed for mass production. Suddenly, Chippendale was out and stainless steel was in.

Fanning the style's popularity was the cinema of the time, which exaggerated its glamour through over-the-top movie sets and costumes in such films as *Our Modern Maidens* (1929) and *Metropolis* (1926). In these and other films of the era, Art Deco is depicted at its most elegant and highly stylized. In fact, movie houses of the time offer the best example of Art Deco at its most atmospheric: created to resemble palaces, with plaster and ornamental wrought iron, the theaters brought the zigzags, murals, mirrors, and lighting of Art Deco style to a whole new level of grandeur, and more importantly, brought this vision of Art Deco to the public.

Even in the highbrow art world, Art Deco left a lasting impression. The posters of artists such as Jean Dupas, who is known primarily for his murals painted for the ocean liner *Normandie*, and A.M. Cassandre, as well as the work of Tamara de Lempicka, lend visual evidence of the impact of Art Deco style. An icon of the Jazz Age, de Lempicka, more than any other artist of the time, captures the era's spirit. In one of her most notable works, *Self-Portrait (Tamara in the Green Bugatti)*, which dates from 1925, de Lempicka is a metaphor for an aesthetic: conscious of its style and certain of its abilities, Art Deco embodies an era that was determined to go places, or at least look as if it did.

Although it was a style seen more frequently in the public realm, Art Deco is nevertheless at home in the home. The style can transform a space, even with a few small, well-placed objects. Ranging from the playful look of the Miami Beach hotels to the sophisticated elegance of New York's Deco landmarks, this book will show you how to capture the spirit of Art Deco style in your home.

LEFT: *One of the finest practitioners of the Art Deco style in the arts was Tamara de Lempicka, a Polish painter. Here, her Portrait of Marquis de'Afflitto (1925), maintains a brooding, sensual quality. In all of her works, the sense of time and place are unmistakably Art Deco.*

CHAPTER ONE

ARCHITECTURE

Drawn from sources ranging from the classical (ancient Greece, Rome, and Egypt) to the futuristic (the space age), to the contemporary (the machine age), Art Deco is a unique amalgamation, combining all the spirit and energy that made up the first decades of the twentieth century in America. And like the era it reflects, Art Deco is everchanging. This may explain why, as a design aesthetic, Art Deco has more exceptions than rules: varying widely by region, the architectural style can be sophisticated (as in many movie theater interiors); whimsical (Miami Beach's strip of hotels); or bold (New York City's skyscrapers).

Most scholars agree, however, that North American Art Deco was at its finest when applied to architecture. Deco buildings emphasize geometry, fluidity, speed, and sophistication. Most of all, they express progress through technology, a major goal of architects, engineers, and designers of the 1920s and '30s. Hence, the style's most recognizable buildings combined machine age and traditional materials: stainless steel, aluminum, glass block, limestone, marble, and terra-cotta.

The birthplace of the skyscraper, New York, is also the architectural center of Art Deco. A New York City zoning law allowed buildings to be built higher if they were set back from the street, so stepped-back skyscrapers flourished in Manhattan. Taking its main influence from the stepped temples of the ancient Egyptian, Mayan, and Aztec cultures, the Art Deco style was eagerly adopted by architects who wanted to build skyscrapers to their maximum height allowance.

Today, this "skyscraper style" is what most people think of when they hear the term "Art Deco architecture." The style, with its vertical decorations and alignment of windows, is meant to draw the eye upward. Features such as zigzag terracing and "racing stripes" (banding that was either painted or created with the placement of spandrels or moldings) were added to buildings to help alleviate the massive look, as well as give them a sleek, rakish quality.

If New York City defines Art Deco for the sophisticated city dweller, then the strip of hotels along Miami's South Beach is the style's vacationing twin sister. More relaxed, whimsical, and far

OPPOSITE: *The best examples of Art Deco architecture are the many public or commercial buildings erected in North America. Here, the Bank of Montreal, in Vancouver, epitomizes the grandeur of the style. The elaborate sun motif, stylized birds, and stepped and zigzag reliefs of the sculpted entrance all point to influences from Aztec culture—a favorite inspiration among architects at the time.*

more colorful than any derivation of Art Deco seen elsewhere in North America or Europe, the hotels and apartment buildings make up what is known as"Tropical Deco."

With predominantly low-rise structures and pastel colors, the strip of hotels in Miami's Art Deco District represents the largest concentration of Art Deco architecture in North America: with some eight hundred buildings in both the Art Deco and Mediterranean Revival styles, the district was aptly named to the National Register of Historic Places in 1979, thanks largely to the efforts of the Miami Design Preservation League.

Drawing on typical Art Deco motifs such as zigzags, the hotels' architects plainly took creative license. Using their local surroundings as both inspiration and backdrop, prolific architects such as Henry Hohauser incorporated native birds, plants, and ocean imagery into their creations. Today, these recurring motifs are the core of Tropical Deco.

Motifs aren't their only unique attributes: "eyebrows" above the windows, etched glass, and rounded corners are only a few exterior eccentricities. There are even Deco hotels that mimic ocean liners, complete with porthole windows, deck rails, and ships' towers! Although many of these buildings are similar in construction to the cool, detached buildings of the Bauhaus school (both styles often incorporated such materials as stucco, glass block, and terrazzo floors), the spirit couldn't be more different than in the big cities.

From New York's renowned skyscrapers to Miami's resplendent Deco hotels, Deco buildings aren't meant to be studied so much as they are meant to be enjoyed.

RIGHT: *With cheerful pastel color combinations and rounded edges, these low-rise Miami Beach hotels, most of which were built in the 1920s and '30s, embody Art Deco at its most playful. In a style nicknamed "Tropical Deco," many of the buildings that line the Miami beachfront were built of stucco and typically adopted nautical themes.*

RIGHT: *A carved—and curved—relief decorates the entrance to this Miami apartment house. The bold horizontal striping and simple lighting fixtures are inspired by Deco's pared-down, futuristic sensibility.*

OPPOSITE: *Even in a traditional setting, Art Deco's influence is unmistakable. Here, a typical Palladian doorway is given new life by the stylized rising-sun motif atop the door. The doorknock and numberplate coordinate with the brassy sun, which offers decorative relief to the too-serious wooden door.*

LEFT: *The stepped shape of this detail of a Tropical Deco hotel is embellished by a sculpted relief awash with a bold combination of color, giving it a playful look.*

OPPOSITE: *A detail of the corner of a Miami Beach hotel shows the kind of metamorphosis Art Deco went through in certain regions of the United States. The same geometric forms and zigzags indicative of traditional Art Deco are made playful by a uniquely Floridian color scheme.*

ABOVE: *This sculpted balcony shows the fluid, clean detailing that is Art Deco's trademark. Stylized flowers carved in bas-relief in the corners complement the grooved columns and angular shape of the balcony.*

ABOVE: *The "wings" atop this Miami Beach building give it a rakish look—something many Art Deco structures have in common. In fact, one of Art Deco's main architectural objectives was to pull the eye upward by using elaborate detailing or artistry atop buildings or on ceilings. This particular building also features stepped sides that are reminders of the style's tribal influences.*

ABOVE: *Art Deco architecture has many influences, including Cubism, the Mayan and Aztec cultures, and most importantly, the Machine age. It is a style like no other.*

ABOVE: *There's no such thing as "too bold" with Miami Beach Art Deco, also known as "Tropical Deco." Here, a canary yellow coat of paint is just the thing to get this façade noticed. For added emphasis, the owners of this building threw in touches of red, purple, and blue in the friezework and the grooved columns. Both details emphasize verticality.*

LEFT: *A massive collaborative effort between developers, architects, and designers, Rockefeller Center in New York City stands as one of the most glorious examples of Art Deco style. Here, a close-up of one of the architectural ornamentations of the International Building at Rockefeller Center shows some motifs common to many structures built during the Jazz Age. These include rays of the sun, stylized flowers, human figures, and animals, as well as ancient Egyptian themes.*

RIGHT: *One of the most widely recognized works of the Art Deco period must be Paul Manship's Prometheus, the sculpture that presides over the fountain at the base of the Channel Gardens at Rockefeller Center in New York City. In the background is another famous Art Deco work, a sculpted relief in front of the RCA building, the tallest of the Center's structures.*

OPPOSITE: *Wild pastel colors come together in Tropical Deco to create a fanciful feel. This type of detail at the top of a Deco building is intended to bring the eye upwards.*

LEFT: *An Art Deco apartment shows an appreciation for sleekness and curves.*

CHAPTER TWO
FURNISHINGS AND INTERIORS

Art Deco furniture today is much sought-after by admirers of the style. In fact, original pieces are rare finds. Much of the furniture that survives was one-of-a-kind, created in the workshops of the best-known French furniture designers of Art Deco's day, including Emile-Jacques Ruhlmann, Louis Süe, André Mare, Pierre Chareau, Edgar Brandt, and Jean Dunand. It was the influence of a number of designers, including Joseph Urban, Paul Frankl, Kem Weber, and Donald Deskey, the designer of Radio City Music Hall's interiors, that led to the distinctive look of American Art Deco furniture.

Furniture makers were also increasingly industrial designers in the 1920s. Norman Bel Geddes, for example, was a New York City theater set designer who had also worked in advertising. He coined the term "industrial designer" when he opened his own design studio in 1927. As an industrial designer, or product engineer, Bel Geddes and his contemporaries, particularly the industrial designer Raymond Loewy, were concerned with instilling products with one attribute above all—streamlining. Hired by the Simmons Company, Bel Geddes designed bedroom furniture that advanced his ideals.

Furniture designs often mirrored architectural forms. For example, Frankl designed terraced bookcases that mimicked the stepped-back forms on skyscrapers. Deskey, too, took inspiration from architecture, even in choosing the construction materials: he used industrial materials such as Bakelite and stainless steel in designing many of his pieces.

The most common trait among Art Deco furniture pieces is that they fit comfortably in a world dominated by machines. Borrowing heavily from the iconography of the day, as well as from ancient cultures, furniture produced in this era continues to provide inspiration for contemporary designers. In today's interior design, there is no lack of Art Deco–influenced furniture.

Art Deco furniture pieces were often a showcase for the period's newest or choicest materials. Made of tubular steel, plastic, "sharkskin" (shagreen), and tinted or frosted glass, the furniture also set itself apart in its construction and finishes. For example, lacquer and tortoiseshell finishes were frequently used finishes for commodes, cabinets, and seating frames. Because curves were so prominent in Art

OPPOSITE: *A chevron-patterned floor lays the groundwork for this dining room full of Art Deco appointments. The dining table features rounded corners and is constructed of curly maple. The chairs, too, have bentwood backs made of maple. The seat upholstery color is cleverly picked·up in the ceramics displayed on the curio cabinet.*

Deco, wood pieces were often molded into rounded outlines, as is the case with a line of chairs produced by a Massachusetts company, Heywood-Wakefield.

Pale woods such as sycamore, bird's-eye maple, walnut, and light oak were used to make cabinetry and tables. Color was often left to the upholstery fabric, ranging in shades from mauve and peach to turquoise and purple. Of course, black and white are common to the Art Deco palette.

Deco-inspired upholstered furniture pieces, including the chaise longue and "easy" chair are standards today. Usually oversized, these pieces often feature boldly patterned fabric and emphasize rounded backs and large, curved arms. New pieces, such as the cocktail cabinet and the coffee table, emerged from this era, and continue to flourish today. Some recognizable standards, such as the circular-sided trolley and chrome-and-glass occasional table with C-shaped base, are also being mass-produced.

Nowhere is Art Deco's mark on the world of furnishings more evident, however, than in lighting. Its influence can be seen in table lamps, wall sconces, floor lamps, and chandeliers. The designs were strikingly modern, even by today's standards. Some of the classics include chain-hung marbled bowl pendant chandeliers; glass-and-chrome shell- or fan-shaped sconces, or wall fixtures; table lamps with opaque glass shades, usually on Lucite-and-chrome stands; and highly stylized female figurines holding globes or supporting shades. Perhaps the Deco era's most famous lighting product is the now-ubiquitous torchère. Featuring an upturned shade that casts light on the ceiling, the torchère is employed by interior designers in almost every conceivable style setting, reminding us just how adaptable Art Deco can be.

LEFT: *The striking combination of light woods and sharp geometric shapes gives this room personality. Neutral upholstery complements the dramatic wood furniture and cabinets. Also, frosted-glass accents, stone walls, and dark floors add texture and contrast to the scene.*

LEFT: *Art Deco rooms often comprise a minimal palette to focus attention on surfaces, textures, and wood grains. In this bedroom, black is used as a foil for all of the objects the owner wished to highlight: the curly maple vanity, the round mirror, and the plush ivory-upholstered chair.*

OPPOSITE: *Art Deco was often a combination of extremes—dark and light, straight and wavy, round and square. In this interior, you can see these combinations at work: the dark furnishings against the light walls; the clean edges of the piano with an undulating top; and the U-shaped chairs pulled up to a lacquer checker table. The cabinet, too, is a study in contrasts, with its claw-like inlay design set against a dark wood grain.*

ABOVE: *A detail of an Art Deco–style modern-day apartment shows how little it takes to produce a sophisticated effect. The cylindrical wall sconces flanking an early 1900s print framed in black lacquer, a retro telephone, and a couple of clocks from the era are enough to lend this wall a jazzy appeal.*

LEFT: *The interplay of dark and light is a hallmark of Art Deco rooms. Here, the dark furniture and chestnut floors arranged in a chevron pattern provide a velvety contrast to stark ivory walls and a brass torchère. Ample sunlight pouring in through French doors, as well as fresh flowers, give the room warmth.*

ABOVE: *The Art Deco feeling comes across in this bedroom through the black lacquer bed and matching bedside tables. The curved chrome night table lamps create a subdued lighting effect. A singular print at the head of the bed, along with a minimalist arrangement on the glass-top coffee table, tie the elements of the room together, creating a relaxing environment.*

ABOVE: *Simplicity is the key in this windowed corner. A oversized reclining chair with chunky curved arms is the dramatic foil for red draperies, T–front hall console, and simple aluminum table lamp. The wallpaper on the far wall echoes the shiny patterned fabric of the chair, uniting the design. A stylized area rug over parquet floor completes the Art Deco feel.*

ABOVE, LEFT: *A touch of Art Deco prevents this bedroom from being too somber; cylindrical wall sconces and the rich grains of the wood from the bed, vanity, and hall table imbue the space with light and warmth. An inlaid design made of mother-of-pearl, a popular Deco material, prominently adorns the foot of the bed and is repeated in both the vanity and table.*

ABOVE, RIGHT: *Fan-shaped accessories on the wall and mirrors that emphasize a vertical look lend glamour to this bedroom. A small table lamp with chrome base throws a soft light in the room, highlighting a simple Deco-era print. The overall effect is one of tranquil elegance.*

OPPOSITE: *The abundant use of sleek expanses of wood, particularly in interior spaces, was one of the most characteristic aspects of the Art Deco style. Here, maple is used on both walls and stairs. To keep the look from being monotonous, the designer arranged large pieces of wood into a pattern of contrasting grains. On the floor, parquet blocks also lend visual interest.*

LEFT: *Rounded forms and soft lighting counterbalance the lines of this bedroom. The mirrored vanity, with its geometric wood inlays and rounded edges, complements other curves in the room, including the arms of the leather chair.*

OPPOSITE: *Art Deco elements in this bedroom, with their smooth outlines and unfussy details, complement more traditional furnishings. The mirrored vanity, the armless chair, the radio console, the unusually colored tiled fireplace, and the mantel clock give this setting a retro appeal.*

LEFT: *A soothing background hue used in combination with neutrals and bold prints captures the essence of Art Deco in this living room. A singular grooved column provides a dramatic foil for two ivory club chairs and a metal Eileen Gray side table seen at right.*

LEFT, TOP: *A pair of Deco-style curvy reclining chairs flanks a matching loveseat, making for a cozy conversation area in this living room. A bay of windows—with a minimalist window treatment—allows light to pour in, highlighting the stained glass inserts along the top. The circular cabinet behind the loveseat is a silhouette typical of the period.*

LEFT, BOTTOM: *In this urban living room, side-by-side reclining chairs, featuring sweeping arms made of highly polished bentwood, look like they're built for speed.*

BELOW: *A Cubist painting hangs over an equally geometric fireplace mantel, setting a Modernist tone for this room. A lighted soffit and a dramatic flower arrangement heighten the grandeur of the setting, while two upholstered sofas facing each other add symmetry. The small chrome Eileen Gray table—a signature of the Art Deco period—provides the room's one industrial-style element.*

ABOVE: *The glow of urn-shaped lights combines with warm wood furnishings and floors to give this room its golden hue. Deco effects are provided by the dazzling inlaid wood floor and the Moderne-looking cabinets. The impact is doubled with mirrored cabinets and walls.*

ABOVE: *The clean, austere look of Bauhaus made a great impression on Art Deco, which is the reason why so many furnishings of both styles look great together. Here, the chrome serving cart makes an ideal companion for metal-accented furniture, such as this tubular-steel framed leather chair, which was designed in the 1920s by Le Corbusier, a well-known practitioner of Bauhaus design principles.*

ABOVE: *Who said Art Deco can't be warm? The amber glow created by the table lamp, torchère and sconces of this room is similar to candlelight—and everything looks better in candlelight. Of course, there's also a "groovy" Deco flair in the dining room chairs, the cabinet, and the upright piano, whose linear motif is continued on the wall in a contrasting border with corner.*

OPPOSITE: *The gleam of highly polished light wood surfaces is a focal point of this Deco dining room. Complemented by matte, neutral upholstery, the wood grain is allowed to take the spotlight. Curved bentwood arms on the chair, rounded table ends, and even a small semicircular ledge also demonstrate Art Deco lines.*

LEFT: *A traditional mantel, featuring elaborately carved moldings, belies this room's Art Deco look: the room's appointments, notably the lighting fixtures and lamps, are more in line with Art Deco sparseness. The torchère, an invention of the Art Deco era, stands prominently in the corner.*

A B O V E: *Typical of the clean, understated look of Art Deco interiors, this dining room features several objects that attest to its influence. The dining table, chairs, and matching cabinet—constructed of dark, rich woods—are marked by rounded corners, smooth surfaces, and virtually no decoration. Geometric shapes—seen in the mirror—also add to the Deco look.*

ABOVE: *Wide horizontal bands adorn both the chairbacks of this dining room set and the matching low china cabinet, making a minimalist statement in wood. As in so many Deco interiors, the furnishings of this one are dramatic enough to carry the room. Made of rich, highly polished cherry, the large pieces of this dining room need little in the way of accessories.*

ABOVE: *This dining room pulls together tribal and urban influences to achieve its swank ambience. Its Deco look comes primarily from the highly polished table with rounded corners and U-shaped base that match the smooth lines of the chairs, which have bentwood backs and slightly flared back legs.*

LEFT: *It's easy to keep a room simple yet elegant with Art Deco elements. Ivory-colored walls get all the kick they need from a single print, while subtle recessed lighting shines down on a glass-top dining table surrounded by lean, contoured wood chairs.*

LEFT: *Lines and circles give this room an Art Deco edge. The modern rug, with its Mondrian-like design sets the linear tone; the base of the plant stand and the chair continue the look. The rounded wall sconce and the circular chrome desk lamp are also Deco-era inventions.*

LEFT: *A uniquely shaped, backlit mirror is the focus of this Moderne Style bathroom. Double pedestal sinks feature subtle banding around their bases, as well as chrome fixtures—both reminiscent of Art Deco detailing.*

OPPOSITE: *This bathroom is made both warm and sophisticated through the use of a few Art Deco elements: the wall sconces, black-and-white marble floor, and rich bird's-eye maple cabinetry and tub surround create a space that's both inviting and chic. The chrome towel rack completes the effect.*

LEFT: *From the cool marble floors to the stylized trompe l'oeil cloud pattern above the tilework, this bathroom is an Art Deco fantasy. Lustrous chrome fixtures and a remarkable shower stall give the room a worldly presence, while the mirror maintains the whimsical effects of the painted clouds in its shape.*

CHAPTER THREE

DETAILS AND MOTIFS

Perhaps no other style is as distinguishable as Art Deco, especially in its details. Rounded forms, an emphasis on geometry, rakish designs, and use of industrial materials combined with exotic fittings or flourishes set this style off from all that preceded it—and all that came after it. In its infancy in North America, Art Deco had many inspirations, including a highly decorative French aesthetic, Art Nouveau, which was characterized by curlicues and stylized nature motifs.

Art Deco also took on the more familiar motifs, such as geometric shapes, often resembling the Cubist ideal; the ziggurat, or stepped temple form, which was taken from ancient cultures; and a variation of this, the arc ziggurat, which resembled a stylized cloud formation.

Sky imagery was popular at this time. Sunburst patterns and lighting bolts were repeated in everything from elevator doors to kitchen appliances. Along with these motifs, half-circles, representing radio or telegraph signals were also used frequently, no doubt a constant reminder of the era's desire to display its technological progress.

The continual streamlining of household objects, including furniture and appliances, meant little or no ornamentation—the form itself was the detail. The Modernist's beloved right angles were displaced by swooping curved corners and the aerodynamic designs so integral to Art Deco.

The imagery of speed was also a factor in the use of animal motifs. Edgar Brandt, a renowned Art Deco sculptor, used creatures such as antelopes and gazelles throughout much of the metalwork he produced. Also popular were deer, ibex, horses, and greyhounds. The animals were the organic representation of Art Deco: exotic, fast, and sleek. Panthers, especially, were a favorite of sculptors, who created life-size pieces for use as cocktail-table bases.

Art Deco's propensity for the exotic didn't stop at its motifs, however. Household objects and interiors were often rendered using exotic materials such as mother-of-pearl, ivory, semiprecious stones, lacquer, enamel, and exotic woods such as ebony. Light wood surfaces, such as bird's-eye maple, sycamore, and walnut, were used liberally throughout Deco interiors, and were almost invariably rounded rather than squared off.

OPPOSITE: *Terrazzo floors, a stylized female statuette, and the three-legged half-moon hall table are all representative of Art Deco. The table's steel legs and rounded appearance accentuate the shape of the mirror placed above it. Often, mirrors like this one were used to visually expand a small Deco space. It's a trick designers still employ today in interiors of all styles.*

Although traditional metals such as bronze and wrought iron continued to be used in Art Deco designs for exteriors, designers such as Brandt popularized their use indoors for tables, lamps, and other furnishings. The era also ushered in the use of precious metals, such as copper, silver, and gold, which, combined with new metal-working techniques, allowed artists of the period to continually reinterpret Art Deco.

Although the color palettes varied widely by locale (pastels were the norm in Miami Beach hotels), Art Deco rooms in the 1920s and '30s often made use of stark contrasts between colors. Pale walls, especially in shades of white and beige, served as the backdrop for shocks of color such as magenta or cobalt. Of course, outside of public spaces, the colors were more toned down. But even these had glitter to them: designers at the time relied on silver, chrome, or steel details to complement subdued shades of cream, beige, gold, and taupe.

Floors were also showstoppers in many public Deco buildings. The most commonly used flooring material at the time, terrazzo, which is made from embedding granite or marble chips in concrete, was also the most expressive. Artists created elaborate, brilliantly colored designs for use in lobbies, hallways, and vestibules.

ABOVE: *The abstract geometric jacquard pattern of the tablecloth lends this otherwise too-soft bedroom an edge. Of course, ivory was a favorite Art Deco color because it worked so well with contrasting color schemes. Contemporary Deco rooms still work best with white or ivory as the foil for dark furnishings or a riot of bold colors.*

OPPOSITE: *This stairwell's balustrade is a nod to Deco-era design, winding seamlessly around a tight corner. The lighting fixtures—a vintage chrome and glass chandelier and industrial-look wall sconce—as well as the mirrored console add to the cool modern ambience.*

For interiors of private spaces, however, polished wood block or parquet flooring was the norm. Rugs placed on top of the floors generally had geometric or animal patterns. Linoleum, which was invented in 1863, also came into wide use at the time because of its low cost. Used in modest homes, Linoleum wasn't just placed in kitchens, however: in colorful, geometric patterns, Linoleum decorated the floors of foyers, living rooms, and even bedrooms.

Textiles made for Art Deco interiors were typically bold, vibrant, and abstract. Although worried at first that the Modernist look represented by Art Deco designs was too trendy, American textile mills were nonetheless producing such carpets and rugs in the 1920s, at the behest of major department stores. These designs played on abstract geometric forms, zigzags, curves, skyscrapers, and even flowers. Many are patterned after designs from the Aztec and Mayan cultures.

RIGHT: *An Art Deco statement greets visitors to this home. The stained glass treatment is both vertical and geometric. Also, the motif shown here—a rising sun with linear beams emanating from it—was a popular one throughout the 1920s and '30s.*

LEFT: *These French doors have a distinctly North American Art Deco feel to them: the stained glass panels show a brilliantly colored geometric design that plays off the colors in the two wicker chairs and the fern. Although wicker is not typical of the era, the curved style of the chairs creates a distinctive Deco silhouette.*

ABOVE: *Art Deco is all about contrast, and this room is a good example of the style. Light and dark woods, metal and wood, and rounded forms and lines all counterbalance each other. Other unique elements include a pagodalike effect created simply with green paint and a stained-glass ceiling above the stairs.*

ABOVE: *The furnishings of the Art Deco era largely emphasize materials and smooth shapes, as is typified by this dresser. Rounded corners flank a middle drawer section that is offset by different wood grains. The overall effect is one of understated luxury.*

ABOVE: *Exotic woods were often used in Art Deco furniture pieces. This cabinet, made of bird's-eye maple, is a perfect touch for an elegant dining room. An area rug with geometric motifs supports the Deco emphasis.*

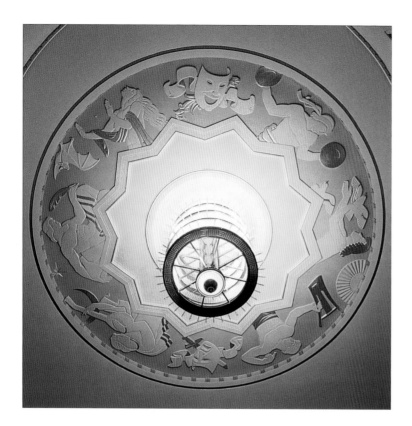

ABOVE: *Bas-relief carvings surrounding this extraordinary ceiling fixture come to life when the light is on: rounded, stylized figures depicting theatrical and musical figures were common motifs used in many Art Deco halls devoted to the arts.*

ABOVE: *This grooved mantel sets the tone for the living space around it. Daring in design, the stucco mantel is accentuated above by two friezes of stylized birds, also Art Deco in influence.*

OPPOSITE: *This carpeted stairwell is a study in drama. A bold, singular design distinguishes the top landing and, one level down, reappears surrounded by a checkerboard pattern. The slinky geometry of the stairs and the stunning carpet design are Deco at its most dashing.*

RIGHT: *The shiny little objects in this room give it a distinctly Art Deco flair. The stand-alone chrome ashtray and tiny aluminum table lamp contrast wonderfully with dark floors and furnishings. Oversized Deco-style coffee cups also add period sophistication to the scene.*

ABOVE: *The sinuous etched lines in this vanity mirror are the telltale sign of Art Deco influence. The reflected surface of the vanity table adds to the glamorous effect.*

CHAPTER FOUR

ACCESSORIES

Because Art Deco interiors are generally spare, accessories are the least recognizable component of the style. Yet, imagine a typical Deco living room without the following items: a stainless steel cocktail shaker, a Bakelite radio, a large mirror with ziggurat-shaped top, a vase from Clarice Cliff. So iconic of Art Deco have these items become that even a non-collector could place them in the proper context. Clocks, small sculpted figurines, glass ornaments, picture frames, and tableware from the era are all easily recognizable.

From René Lalique's most delicate glass perfume bottle to Homer Laughlin's industrial-strength Fiestaware, Art Deco had an impact on the design of accessories made by both man and machine. While fine artists, such as silversmith Jean Puiforcat, continued to create unique pieces for a luxury market, mass production made Deco pieces more affordable to the general public. In fact, one of the most recognizable traits of the Deco style—streamlining—grew out of the industrial designer's desire to create cost-efficient and modern-looking products. As a result, even the most mundane household appliances, such as the radio and the vacuum cleaner, were given natty, streamlined looks, replete with Deco flourishes such as zigzags and racing stripes.

Radios and kitchen utensils were often made with materials such as chrome or nickel-plated steel, painted base metal, a wide range of plastics, and mirrored glass. Usually, they appeared in jazzy color combinations or pastels recaptured on Miami's Deco hotels. And, in a bow to Art Deco architecture, almost all brand-name radios of the time—Air King, Philco, RCA, and Zenith to name a few—were housed in cabinetry that mimicked the Deco façades of the skyscrapers.

The glass industry was also changing to meet the aesthetic standards set by Deco and the economic demand of a growing middle class. By the 1920s, glass makers found new and cheaper ways of producing their wares. Although glass makers such as Orrefors/Kosta Boda, Baccarat, and Steuben came to prominence in the Art Deco period for their art glass, it is the later, mass-produced glass items, such as Depression Glass, that most people associate with the era.

Glass sculptures, however, more fully realized Art Deco's sensibilities. Glass artists, notably Emile Gallé and René Lalique, relied on standard imagery of the time—sleek, urbane women, usually nude; floral and leaf motifs; birds; or geometric abstracts. The largely organic forms complemented the linear look of many Deco interiors.

OPPOSITE: *A sleek female figure was often found at the base of lamps and lighting fixtures produced in the early 1900s. Though created more than seventy years ago, this sculpture lends itself easily to any modern setting.*

Ceramics of the period also indicate the wide swath that Art Deco cut: examples of the style can be found in everything from high-quality china and porcelain to earthenware pottery. Perhaps one of the most well-known of the ceramics that emerged is Fiestaware, a colorful and popular line of dinnerware designed by Homer Laughlin in 1936. Produced continuously from 1936 to 1972, and reintroduced in 1986, Fiestaware led the wave of inexpensive ceramics with Deco styling. Its original colors, ranging from red, blue, yellow, green, ivory, and turquoise, echo Art Deco's bold palettes. Simple circular grooves along the rims of plates, saucers, and cups—usually the only ornamentation in the dinnerware—lend distinction.

Of all household accessories, however, the cocktail shaker best captures the attitude of conviviality and functionality that is at the heart of Art Deco. Designers created a whole host of accoutrements for preparing, serving, and drinking cocktails, not the least of which was the cocktail shaker. Wrought in both aluminum and stainless steel, the cocktail shaker is swank and sophisticated, easily mixing form and function. Ultimately, it's what Art Deco was all about.

LEFT: *The muse for many sculptors of the Art Deco era was the female body, and these pieces are typical of the period. The larger artwork is dramatically displayed against the plain backdrop of a white wall in a lighted alcove. (From the collection of Dennis Wilhem/Michael Kirneck Collection)*

OPPOSITE: *A golden light emanates from this unusual glass torchère. With a design straight from Deco's heyday, this lighting staple is utilitarianism disguised as refinement.*

LEFT: *An advertising poster from 1928 expresses the streamlining so widely used in the graphic arts of the period. The poster combines the impressive imagery of a luxury ocean liner with bold swaths of color and chunky sans-serif type.*

A B O V E : *The book jacket of the Berlin edition of Thea von Harbour's* Metropolis *clearly defines the influence both Art Deco and Bauhaus had on the arts at the time, particularly the graphic arts and the cinema. The cover illustration gives a human face smooth, machine-like characteristics.*

R I G H T : *The mantel was an important element in Art Deco living rooms. Here, illumination is provided not by a roaring fire, but by unusual lighting: a small round glass fixture atop a metal base glows in the mirror placed behind it. The glass block fixtures are fiery as well. (From the collection of Dennis Wilhem/Michael Kirneck Collection)*

TOP, LEFT: *This sleek side table designed by Eileen Gray in the late 1920s is representative of the International Style, which emerged at the same time as Art Deco. Yet, the grouping of objets d'art that the table holds is all Deco, from the pottery and stylized glasswork to the nude statuette.*

BOTTOM, LEFT: *A few well-placed accessories are all it takes to give a bland corner some Art Deco panache. The cocktail shaker—the definitive Deco accessory—along with a few martini glasses and tumblers are attractive accents to the books and other personal effects atop this cabinet.*

OPPOSITE: *The chevrons and curves of this gilt eagle's wings are telltale signs of an Art Deco heritage. It sits on a similarly gilt mantel, which features Egyptian symbols carved in bas-relief; overall, the setting is a stunning focal point for the living room. Furnishings are kept simple with ivory-colored upholstery and light woods.*

LEFT: *Colorful ceramics, à la Fiestaware, have made a huge comeback in the 1990s. Here, pieces from the original Homer Laughlin Fiestaware line are stacked haphazardly: it's hardly messy, though—the rainbow of colors matches well with the mosaic tilework. (From the collection of Cesar Trasobares)*

RIGHT: *In the world of Art Deco ceramics, English ceramist Clarice Cliff embodies the period like no other. Her work often featured bold designs highlighted by brilliant flashes of color and forms inspired by Cubism and Fauvism. Here, a collection of her works is well-displayed in a lighted, built-in shelf.*

ABOVE: *Art Deco's influence extended well past the period in which the style flourished. Here, a vignette of 1950s memorabilia shows several Deco elements, including Fiesta dinnerware and a Bakelite radio.*

LEFT: *Give a bare wall a shot of color—without painting. Here, a display of ceramics in every imaginable shape and size is unified by their one commonality, the color blue. With hues ranging from cornflower to teal, these pieces—reminiscent of the bright colors of Fiestaware, Art Deco–era ceramics created by the Homer Laughlin Company—are a soothing eyeful when grouped together.*

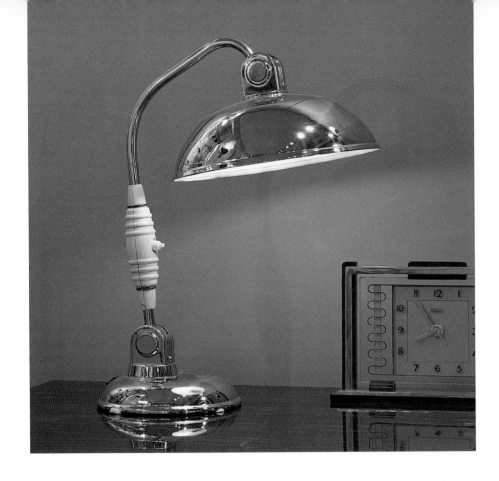

LEFT: *Made of a favorite material of the day, aluminum, this highly polished bedside table lamp is ideal in a room with modern furnishings and accessories. Bright enough for reading at night, it continues to shine even when turned off. The table clock, too, recalls Deco-era ingenuity. The Great Depression forced designers to look at cost-effective industrial materials such as aluminum, chrome, and brass for use in designing products for the home.*

RIGHT: *The table lamp and coffee service shown here evidence Art Deco styling in their use of materials as well as in their shapes. All are rounded, with little ornamentation, and have an industrial feel to them.*

OPPOSITE: *Whether used to shed light on a subject or to be the subject itself, these lamps perform beautifully. They're typical of Art Deco sleekness and sophistication, with grooved edges on the light head that play off the rounded forms they illuminate.*

LEFT: *Bentwood doors, chrome handles and knobs, and a "hood" that lifts to reveal a turntable all lend distinction to this 1930s-designed radio console. As with many industrial designs created in the Jazz Age, this one features streamlined contours and unusual combinations of materials.*

OPPOSITE: *A vintage French Art Deco poster is the main attraction above an elaborate marble mantel. Yet, the demure glass lamps on the mantel, matching statuette candleholders, and the friezework and sinuous columns of the mantel all offer homage to the Art Deco style. (From the collection of Dennis Wilhem/Michael Kirneck Collection)*

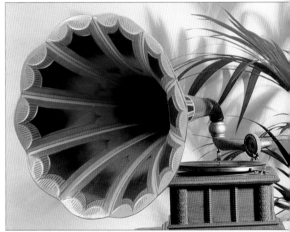

BELOW: *Looking more like a wild lily, this gramophone is a real standout. Its flower-shaped speaker and dramatic color contrasts add to its Art Deco flavor.*

LEFT, TOP: *This bas-relief—of the Roman goddess of the hunt, Diana—forms a large medallion, offering a sophisticated look to the plaster fireplace hood. Off to the side is an unusual circular table lamp with a hanging fixture. Indicative of Deco designers' penchant for using industrial materials such as chrome and aluminum for household objects, the lamp is an ideal accompaniment to this interior.*

LEFT, BOTTOM: *Sweeping curves are often the stamp of Moderne influence, evident in this cabinet with black panthers slinking across its top. The bronze statuettes complement the grooved black accents of the piece and contrast nicely with the polished wood finish.*

OPPOSITE: *Its cool serenity made marble an ideal building material during the Art Deco period. In fact, it was often used to create small household objects, such as this mantel clock. Other details, including a stepped, geometric form, sans-serif type, and nude figurine, lend Deco distinction.*

PHOTOGRAPHY CREDITS

Front and back jacket photography: Elizabeth Whiting and Associates

Abode: 47, 53, 60 left

AKG: 83 left

Arcaid: ©Ken Kirkwood: 94 bottom; ©Nick Meers: 12 (Architect: Oliver Hill; Sculptor: Eric Gill)

Art Resource, NY: 15

©Steven Brooke Studios: 11 (Architect: L. Murray Dixon), 20 (Architect: Robert Collins), 22, 24 left, 44, 74 right, 80, 81, 83 right, 86, 93 left

©Edifice/Dunnel: 25 left

©Edifice/Lewis: 24 right, 28, 29

Elizabeth Whiting and Associates: 39, 46 both, 60–61 (Architect: Hebert C. Rhodes), 62, 73 right; ©Peter Aprahamian: 71, 78; ©John-Paul Bonhommet: 35, 56, 69, 73 left, 84 top, 90, 91 both, 92, 95; ©Nick Carter: 57 (Designer: Paul Tierney); ©Eric Crichton: 64–65 (Country House Hotel); ©Brian Harrison: 63; ©Clive Helm: 5 (Architect: Adrian Jones); ©Rodney Hyett: 54 left; ©Tom Leighton: 30; ©Di Lewis: 70, 87; ©Neil Lormier: 7; ©Tim Street-Porter: 40 right (Architect: Piers Gough); ©Spike Powell: 42, 49 (Owner: Helen Ward), 59 right, 76; ©Andreas von Einsiednel: 43, 45 top, 45 bottom (Designer: Mary Fox Linton)

©Phillip H. Ennis: 32–33, 48, 58 (Designer: Jean-Paul Viollet)

Envision: ©Bart Barlow: 10; ©Michael Kingsford: 8

©Tria Giovanni: 27, 84 bottom

©Nancy Hill: 37 (Designer: Stuart Witt)

©image/dennis krukowski: 75 (Metropolitan Home Show House)

The Interior Archive: ©Simon Brown: 36–37, 50–51, 52, 77; ©Fritz von de Schulenburg: 40 left, 54–55

Leo de Wys: ©Angelo Cavalli: 25 right; ©Clifford Hausner: 23; ©Henryk T. Kaiser: 13; ©J. Messerschmidt: 26; ©Siegfried Tanquer: 18–19

Photobank: ©Vanderschuit Studios: 85

©Eric Roth: 34, 38, 41 (Designer: C & J Katz Studio), 59 left, 68 (Designer: Geib Truesdale Interior Design), 72 (Designer: Rick Garafola), 89

Superstock: 16, 21, 82, 93 right

Unicorn Stock Photography: ©Aneal F. Vohra: 74 left

©Jesse Walker: 2, 66, 88–89, 94 top